NOBODY TO LIFT ME

A STORY OF FAITH, HOPE, LOVE & REDEMPTION

Just as the pyramids were lifted up and gave rise to a great people ...

MoDear gave rise to a strong legacy of love for her family!

SOURCES

Book Design by Virginia Hall-Broadnax

Illustrations: Free Clip Art from the I-Net

Photos from the Author's & Other Family Member's Scrapbooks

NOTE: There are several instances where words are purposely Misspelled to use a certain vernacular.

****

To Order additional books please visit Amazon.com or contact the author at mirrorofdreams@cox.net or
FACEBOOK @ Virginia Hall-Broadnax

FROM HUMBLE BEGINNINGS

Highway 82 East

Union Springs (Bullock County), Alabama

****

Special Thanks To:

Mr. David Jeffers, who gave of his time and invaluable assistance through formatting and overall publishing of my manuscript; Visit him on the website at: 7ps2authorship.com

Ms. LaToya Loveless, author of "I Moved Out ... Now What? -- For invaluable information and encouragement.

Two beautiful ladies who spent time proofreading
(Ms. Mable Hughes-Bostic, niece;
Ms. Mattie Jackson, sistah-friend – I love you ladies).

WHERE I'VE BEEN

LIVED **

ALABAMA (Union Springs) **	MISSISSIPPI
ARIZONA	MISSOURI
ARKANSAS	NEVADA
COLORADA	NEW JERSEY
FLORIDA (Ft. Walton Beach; Miami) **	NEW YORK
GEORGIA (Decatur, Stone Mountain, Lithonia) **	NORTH CAROLINA
ILLINOIS (Chicago) **	OHIO
INDIANA	PENNSYLVANIA
KANSAS	SOUTH CAROLINA
KENTUCKY	TENNEESEE
LOUISIANA	VIRGINIA
MARYLAND	WASHINGTON D.C.
MICHIGAN	WISCONSIN
MINNESOTA	GHANA, WEST AFRICA; NASSAU, BAHAMAS

In Loving Memory of

My mother, Julia Mae "MoDear" Tolbert Hall (1906-1995), for her unconditional love, devotion to family, rich legacy of sharing, caring, and for teaching me how to always "have faith in God". **And**

My daddy, SSgt. "Tuff/Strawberry" (1910-1969) who died much too young. Daddy, I never truly understood and appreciated the trials of a Black man of your generation until I became of age. **And**

My sister Rosemary, who was a surrogate mother and protector for my son and I; words can't describe how much I love her and appreciate all the things she shared and taught me. She was always there for us through "thick and thin". I can still hear her saying "It's all good" and you know what – it has never been better! **And**

My sister Lillian (PeeWee), who marched to her *own* drummer; loved to dance and always had a way of drawing you into her world! **And**

My Uncle Andrew Tolbert, who enjoyed life to the fullest especially through his Bridge games and travel. **And**

My Uncle John "Doc" Hudson, who loved himself some White Port and his "Angel Baby" (me). **And**

My maternal Grandmother "Sweet Tolbert" who made *chewing* gum a work of art, and man she made that old leather strap hurt! **And**

My maternal Grandfather "Papa" who was a "wannabe" ladies and mojo man. **And**

My niece Angela Eve (Punkin), who was beautiful and carefree. **And**

My first-born nephew Alfred, who was so talented in carpentry. When I think of what could've been – man! Another time and place Deke! **And**

My nephew, Mangano "Tree" who left a legacy of giving unselfishly to the young boys and girls (coaching basketball) and no matter how much pain he was in, he never complained. He was famous for his culinary skills and his "McGuyver" skills (Mr. Fix-It). He is irreplaceable!

And to all the others who left the struggle too soon I say *"A Luta Continuum! (The struggle must continue)"*.

ACKNOWLEDGEMENTS - FAMILY

Mr. "B", if you only knew the depth of me. I have witnessed God work a miracle in your life and He has prepared you to walk a different path (favor). Terence (Tiger) you have always made me proud to be your mother (you are a rare jewel). Jennefir (BG), you have stolen a big chunk of my heart - you are truly my daughter. Ella (no greater love than you; I can still remember when you disciplined me as a child and I dare not "sass" you – even now).

Bettye, it was fun growing up with you - we were some mischievous chirren. Peaches, I don't know anybody in your age bracket who can throw down in the kitchen like you. Marcus (by God's grace - talk about transformation - favor has invaded your territory; God is awesome. Gretta and Darryl - you were there for MoDear and me when it mattered the most; Darryl, I can always count on you for an intellectual and stimulating conversation. CJ, thanks for our special bond and for touching and understanding that place in my soul that was too painful to share with anyone but you (I AM GLAD God's prophecy won out over a man's). "Lady" Di, you are a devoted & sexy grandma – gull (sic) I wanna be like you when I grow up.

Bonnie your generosity is phenomenal and your decorating/carpentry skills rival some of those professionals on HGTV; thanks for always spoiling me (it's all good"). Willie "Bosco" Bostic, you are so talented (tailor, expert fisherman, and inventor – love you man). Tonya you are blessed with some dope decorating skills; B. J., you never cease to amaze me with your wit and humor and phenomenal photography. Tony, thank you for your Marine service amidst all the turmoil and bigotry you endured; according to Genesis 1:27 "God created man in his own image, in the image of God he created him"; He's your Father. Jerry "when a man finds a wife, he finds a good thing - Johnetta". Maurice, man you never let it get you down – keep the faith.

Mary, girl you are blessed beyond measure; it was a long time coming but you made it! Theresa, dreams do come true; we all have secret spaces where we feel safe- you were supposed to be a choreographer - sidetracked. Alonza, your culinary skills are a work of art; you got jokes too. Regina, you are the epitome of courage. Pat, you are a blessing to all who know your story. Pleshette, you are a talented wheeler/dealer. Sandy, blessings kept you. Chauncey, we all have overcome by the Grace of God. Jayson and "Nick" you have both risen to the occasion of becoming productive young men in your chosen professions; I am so proud of you for your tenacity (I wish we were not so far apart; when I look at you, I thank God for your Mom MaryJo and Dad Terence, who taught you respect and tolerance).

Marcus R – I am so proud of you and your accomplishments - go on wit 'yo bad sef (sic). Taylor I am so proud of you ("teach them well and show them the way"). "Ree, thanks always for your commitment to MoDear. April, Latoya and Amber, you are beautiful inside/out (you have proven that young Black Women can rise up and accomplish dreams and goals that others are afraid to tackle)! Broadnax Family (especially JB's siblings).

I LOVE YOU ONE & ALL

ACKNOWLEDGEMENTS - FRIENDS

To friends who have often told me – "Jenny, you are blessed - you are a walking miracle and you have so much to give." For those words of encouragement, I say thank you!

My heart goes out to my dearest friends, Rev. Ted "Pops" and Lynette Walker who have proved repeatedly that you are the epitome of love unconditional. You have always supported me and believed in me when sometimes I didn't have the strength to believe in myself.

Mattie Jackson, Sistah/friend; thanks for making me laugh and understanding that whatever we confront – we can always agree that "it's not that serious" LOL). Janice McReynolds you are the best traveling partner and roommate in the world – love our bond. Lillie Alford-Loggins & Glenda Alford-Atkins, thanks always for listening, understanding and encouraging me in the early transition stages of my moving here to FWB – my heart will forever be linked to you in a forever Sistah bond. Evangelist Pamela Crowell, you are my "fireball" preacher/teacher; Eatha Marshall, you were a FANTASTIC MOD Mentor with a beautiful spirit.

Jackie Allen, Peaches Coleman, Denise Henderson, Rosie Saunders, Wanda Carney, and Sharon Miller, (ATL VAMC-HEC employees/friends who treated me like family); Minister Evergreen Freeman, Rev. PJ & Minister Sammie Walker (forever friends); Dr. Chlotia Posey-Garrison (the most non-critical and committed person I know).

Pastor & Mrs. Thigpen (Papa & Mama "T") of Beulah FB Church (thanks for your leadership). My General Mission Sisters - you ladies ROCK! Rosetta Faulkner-Draper one of MoDear's caretakers - THANKS. Julia Shannon Green I will always cherish the personal and working relationship we shared for years (your kids – especially Yolanda was like my child).

Rev. Elect Lady Debery Washington - Sistah/Girlfriend forever. Cassandra Morrison, somebody's gotta teach 'em. Mt. Olive Church Family and the late Pastor James Bass (who spoke life to me – "Daughter, you don't have to go through that"). Rev. Kenneth Giles who referred to me as his "radical preacher" – thanks Pastor Giles. House of Light Church Family - Apostle & Prophetess Thornton - great teachers and expounders of the Word, (I learned a lot from the two of you); Bonnie Shines Fourte I love you Lady from High School to now!

Mother Arlethia Gilliam (you give new meaning to the term – entrepreneur). Rhonda Benton – you are richly blessed with God's favor (I have seen the Prayer of Jabez, come to fruition in your life). First Missionary Baptist Church USA and Pastor Gary Lewis, you are a blessing to the community and young people. I am so grateful to you for entrusting the Youth to my care and trusting me enough to preach the WORD.

SPECIAL SHOUTOUTS: Beulah Youth & Ministry Staff; Sandra Gainey; Mercedez Claybrone; Mary Mercer-Jordan; Joyce Ponder; Stan & Jean Kennedy; Renishia Richardson; Korena Jones-Brown; My'Onna Pride; Eleanor Johnson Youth Center Staff; Pasha Cunningham; Rev. Felix Cole; Elder Dexter Scott; Rev. & Mrs. Peter Doe; Deacon & Mrs. Eugene Jackson; Rev. & Mrs. Willie Farrow; Harry "Rap" Brown; Doris Scaife; Deacon & Mrs. Richard Parker; Montis Wilson (I am so proud of you for connecting with the King inside of you; stay focused).

I LOVE YOU ONE & ALL

CONTENTS

INTRODUCTION

Nobody to Lift Me was inspired by the life, legacy, pain and suffering of the author's mother, Julia "MoDear" M. Tolbert Hall and the author herself.

"MoDear" was a visionary who was, *in my eyes*, way ahead of her time. Through her wisdom, she taught her family how to give, how to love and above all how to have faith. She used to always tell me, "If I had had (sic) somebody to lift me up, ain't no telling what I could have been -- I didn't have nobody to lift me up." However, it was not until years later that I would truly understand what these simple but very profound words meant.

Therefore, MoDear, through this book, I lift you up and through your legacy of love, caring, sharing, and self-empowerment, your family is also lifted up!

"If I be lifted up from the earth I will draw all men unto me."

John 12:32   (Holy Bible, King James Version)

MoDear was born into a family of four sisters and five brothers and was plagued with many "afflictions" throughout her childhood. She contracted scarlet fever when she was a child, and as a result, suffered a very severe ear infection (left untreated by a medical doctor) that would ultimately lead to her becoming completely deaf.

As others born to greatness can attest, MoDear did not let those afflictions deter her. She would later rise to greatness in the eyes of those who loved and respected her and she would leave a legacy of trials and triumphs.

When I read Proverbs 31, I am reminded of my mother who was strong, and had the ability to do things that almost seemed impossible when I look back over our lives. MoDear was the epitome of a virtuous woman even before I knew what it meant!

This Proverb describes my mother as if it were written personally for her:

"A good woman is hard to find, and worth far more than diamonds.

She shops around for the best yarns and cottons, and enjoy knitting and sewing.

She's like a trading ship that sails to faraway places and brings back exotic surprises.

She's up before dawn, preparing breakfast for her family and organizing her day.

She looks over a field and buys it, then, with money she's put aside, plants a garden. First thing in the morning, she dresses for work, rolls up her sleeves, eager to get started. She senses the worth of her work, is in no hurry to call it quits for the day.
She's skilled in the crafts of home and hearth, diligent in homemaking.

She's quick to assist anyone in need, reaches out to help the poor. She doesn't worry about her family when it snows; their winter clothes are all mended and ready to wear. She makes her own clothing, and dresses in colorful linens and silks.

She keeps an eye on everyone in her household, and keeps them all busy and productive. Her children respect and bless her; charm can mislead and beauty soon fades. The woman to be admired and praised is the woman who lives in the Fear-of-God. Give her everything she deserves!"

Proverbs 31 (The Message Bible)

Just like that virtuous woman described in **Proverbs 31**, MoDear, knitted hats & vests from yarn; made quilts & made clothes (sold her creations in the community); Was an excellent cook; Purchased property when it was not popular for women to own property in their names; Planted huge fields and gardens and peddled produce from door-to-door; Worked as a homemaker and worked in the health-care field as a midwife; Helped those who were not as blessed as herself; Her family and friends respected her and blessed her and without a doubt, she feared God!

Who can find a
virtuous woman?
for her price is
far above rubies.
Proverbs 31:10

FAMILY DEVOTION: Do the Right Thing & Love Each Other

MoDear thrived on telling her children and grandchildren, "Y'all better do the right thing, love God and love each other." She believed in family and she believed in her God. There were times when we did not always do the right thing but somewhere in the back of our minds, we knew that MoDear's praying spirit was intervening – lifting us all up to God to encourage us *to do* the right thing. Even though MoDear had a limited formal education (she only went to the eighth grade), she was steeped in "mother wit."

She understood the value of family and she knew that our African roots dictated that a mother's job was to educate and nurture her children. MoDear always wanted her family to love each other and treat each other with dignity and respect – a lesson often forgotten in today's society. We may not have always heeded her voice but all who knew her can attest to the fact that if you knew MoDear, you had to have come in contact with her take on "loving, caring and sharing."

Now don't get me wrong! I am not trying to paint a picture here of a perfect woman. MoDear had her faults like everybody else. She had some cuss words I still do not know to this day, what they mean. What is a *son-of-a-damn-cram?* (LOL) She could fuss – man could she fuss. Get on a topic and would wear it out. ***Babeee!***

But I can tell you this, she sure knew what she was talking about when she told us something and most of the time we could take it to the bank - couldn't we "Simpie"? Girl you know what I'm talking about. Remember the time that dude came to see you in that storm and MoDear told you, *"Girl you got something on your hands, you ain't gonna (sic) be able to get rid of."* Was she right or what? Scary!

Even though MoDear could work *our* nerves and *hers* at the same time, the love she showed in the meantime could overshadow those negatives and we loved her in spite of all that fussing. Even today, the Hall Family -even though we don't' always agree on some things - love each other and we dare you to mess with one of our clan, honey you got a fight on your hands!

I do not know when MoDear took on the role of official caregiver in the family. However, I can remember when I was a young girl, how she would travel to different houses and take care of aunts, uncles, grandmother, grandfather, cousins – you name them. I can remember traveling on the train to Troy, Alabama with my mother to see Sis. Lil when she was *"feeling poorly"*. Then I can remember her moving in with Mama (grandma Sweet Tolbert) to take care of her. She moved Papa (grandpa Tolbert) in with us. She took care of her Aunt Daughter, kept an eye on her Aunt Babe and many others I can't even remember. She used to tell me, *"Baby, I done just about waited on everybody in the family."*

MoDear was a chosen vessel and even though "walking in purpose" was not a phrase we heard or understood back then, MoDear was walking in her purpose. Her steps were divinely ordered by the Lord and she exemplified Luke *12:48, "...For everyone to whom much is given, of him shall much be required."* MoDear was given much spiritually! She lived on a very small, fixed income but she paid her bills on time, paid her tithes, gave money to the "grands" and others for birthdays, holidays and special occasions.

I still to this day cannot fathom how she made it; on second thought, yes I can - it is because she was unselfish with her gifts and the fact that she gave back to the Lord what He had blessed her with – that's how she was able to make it. It was through MoDear' s generosity and giving spirit that I learned that "the more you give, the more you receive" and to this day, that still holds true for me.

MAGIC IN DEM THERE HANDS

Quilting

To this day, my family and I still have quilts that MoDear pieced together, framed and put together into beautiful works of art. I often look at some of these quilts and am reminded of dresses, and other pieces of clothing I used to wear. Needless to say, some of the memories evoked by these pieces of fabric are bittersweet.

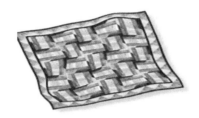

Sewing

I don't care what the occasion was, we could always count on MoDear to rise to the challenge of putting together a designer's original. Graduation dress – wedding dress, you name it! All I had to do was describe to her what I wanted my outfit to look like and she would have it made without delay. Okay so do you think I always appreciated those originals? No! What I wouldn't give today to have that kind of talent and some of those one-of-a-kind designs!

MoDear was gifted and all she needed was ***someone to lift her up***! To appreciate and understand her God-given talent and her never-ending capacity to love!

Similar pattern of my high school graduation dress (made by MoDear)

Carpentry

I never met anyone, let alone a woman who could build furniture until I saw my MoDear build a bed. I'm telling you, she was no pushover! That bed was heavy and withstood all the abuse we put it through! If I seem a little biased, I am!

MoDear was my shero, my role model, my foundation and my reason for wanting to have a bright future. She was truly before her time and we failed to see it back then!
And for that MoDear, I now *lift you up* to your rightful place. A place of honor, a place of dignity, a place of respect, a place of thankfulness and a place of high esteem through God who does all things well!

Culinary Delights

MoDear was an excellent cook who could make a delicious meal out of the simplest ingredients. Even though we were "poor" by some standards, I can never remember being hungry a day in my life growing up.

We had fresh vegetables, fresh chickens, wild game (you couldn't pay me to eat 'possum' today) and all the fixings that were plentiful from the garden.

My MoDear was an artist when it came to cooking. She made biscuits from scratch on the fireplace and the most beautiful roasted sweet potatoes in the fireplace ashes. We were blessed beyond measure and we didn't have a clue!

HARD WORK NEVER KILLED NOBODY

- ° Working In the Fields From Can To Can't

- ° Peddling Produce

- ° Homemaker

- ° Wife, mother and grandmother who ran her household well

- ° Domestic Worker (worked in other's homes cooking, cleaning and babysitting)

- ° Licensed Midwife

- ° Cook (worked in the kitchen of the local hospital in our hometown)

- ° Foster Grandmother (in a Day Care Center as a City of Chicago surrogate grandmother)

MoDear loved to see things grow and always planted a garden every year. She was born on a farm and her life revolved around growing vegetables to preserve by putting them in jars and by selling vegetables from door to door.

I hated it when I had to chop the weeds away from the vegetables. In my wish to get through quicker, I would sneak and chop some down (I know – bad girl)! Even more so, I hated knocking on those "doors" knowing we had to go to the back. But when it came to feeding her family, my mother's love for us, took a back seat to her having to go to the back door.

MoDear would get up early to get her work done at home and get ready for an eight-hour day at the local hospital, health department, or at private homes. Whatever the task at hand, she was always up for the challenge.

She would always tell us, **"Hard work ain't never killed nobody".** If it didn't, why was I soooo tired when *I* had to work! She would say, **"I always worked from 'can to can't' but y'all can't take nothing."**

My sisters who were all older than me, would go to work at my uncle's farm but since I was the "baby", I escaped that chore (didn't know how to pick cotton, picked some peas sometime but mostly just got in my sisters' way).

And they never let me forget – always telling me, **you just spoiled, MoDear used to kill us."** I was like she be killing me too!

NOTE: From can to can't - start early in the morning and stop when you can't see daylight!

EDUCATION: "Stay in School So You Can Be Somebody"

These words became a mantra I would hear sooooooooo many times from MoDear. She believed that educating her children would become their gateway out of poverty and generational curses. She wanted so very badly for us to achieve something that had always been out of *her* reach.

MoDear had dreams and ambitions of becoming a nurse but she did not have the financial means nor the support of her family to accomplish those dreams. That's why she tried so hard to give us the best education possible. MoDear taught us humility while instilling in us, strength and how to look toward the future). She taught us that, "**Knowledge puffs up, but love builds up.**" **I Corinthians 8:1**

Even though I did not complete the first leg of my college career, until I was 32 years old, MoDear was able to witness me walk across that stage and *man* was she a happy soul on that long-awaited night.

I now know that obtaining an education does not necessarily mean that you will be somebody (I know a lot of educated folks who are totally messed up), but I am so grateful that MoDear saw the value in *me* getting a college degree.

For those of us who are Believers, we know that the real education comes from knowing God and living in the power of His might. Nevertheless, **I AM** because MoDear saw my worth and she understood the destiny that God had ordained for me while I was still in her womb (she would so often say to me **"you are my last hope"**).

As a result of the lessons MoDear taught me, I've always tried to instill in young people, how important it is for them to have DREAMS and rise up to their fullest potential (some listened, some didn't). Nevertheless, I will never give up on them!

Below is an excerpt from a letter I wrote to one of the young men I mentored in my Not-for-Profit Organization (Mirror of Dreams Workshop, Inc., a Rites of Passage Program), while he was incarcerated; that's why we should work extraordinarily hard so they don't wind up in these places! (Name has been changed):

August 24, 2008

Dear Harrison,

How are you? I am doing great. I am writing to say I hope you are doing ok (in spite of your present circumstances) and to encourage you to do your best while you are there in Rantoul. I hope you don't become bitter and give up.

Harrison, I was always drawn to you because I could see the great potential you have to be a leader. However, you must take a step outside of yourself and look within to see what God has planned for your life. You have everything readily available in your life but you must be willing to set some goals and give your life a worthwhile meaning. You were not born to be a loser but you were created to make a positive difference in your community and in the world.

When I was there in Chicago, I always had you guys' best interest at heart because too many young brothas wind up just walking without purpose.

Take a look around you and decide that you don't want to be just another statistic; another young Black man without an education; another young man behind bars or stretched out in a coffin.

Harrison, you owe it to yourself and to those who will come after you, to take a stand for what is right and take your rightful place. You need to prepare yourself by being all you can be by getting a quality education and preparing yourself for the future. God wants you to be successful and He wants to give you a good life.

As you continue on your journey in life, remember what **Jeremiah 29:11** *says; "For I know the plans I have for you," declares the Lord, "plans to prosper you and not to harm you, plans to give you hope and a future."* So let go Harrison and let God guide every decision and step you make okay? You already know that you are made in God's image and because God is great, you are great. Set some goals for your life and never ever stop **DREAMING!**

I love you and I believe in you and what you can become. Your being in Rantoul is only a minor setback to get you on the right track (use it to your benefit and don't goof off while you are there). Be blessed and always know that God loves you and He will never ever give up on you **DREAMER!** Always in your corner! **Ms. Virginia**

DREAMS & VISIONS: Like Mother, Like Daughter

Sometimes listening to MoDear could be downright scary when she started talking about her "dreams and visions." It was like, "MoDear, please do not dream *ANYTHING* about me!" We did not want to be in her dreams and we sure did not want her to dream about fish! When she dreamed about fish, man you could bet your life that somebody in the family was "pregnant" -- it never failed.

I was very young but I can remember as if it was yesterday – the profoundness of one of her visions. MoDear told us about the time her brother Brown was killed. She told her mama and papa and the rest of her family that she had seen his death but nobody would believe her; that is until the police rode up to the house and told them Brown had been killed - just like MoDear had seen it. Man, she had the *"gift"*.

Then there was the time MoDear was asleep and she was talking in her sleep. She was telling one of her great grandchildren, Cedric – "boy take that thing out yo mouth". **I was standing next to her and I nudged her awake and asked her: "MoDear, who were you talking to? She said, "Cedric had a safety pin in his mouth and he swallowed it". Man, talk about prophetic, it was just a few days later that Cedric swallowed** a safety pin and almost choked! By this time, of course, we were all like – **PLEASSSSE do not dream anything about me PLEASSSSE!!!**

Now that the baton has been passed on to me, dreams and visions have become a part of who I am. Some of my family members have told me, "Tee" **pleasse (notice I am not in MoDear's league yet)** don't dream anything about me. But as fate would have it – how come I am now in the clique?

Some years ago while living in Chicago, I dreamed that the police came up on our front porch and found a gun. They met two women walking down the sidewalk, stopped them and told them, they had found a gun on their porch.

Low and behold, two weeks later two policemen went up on our porch searching for a gun (they did not find it but it was there, hidden under some debris); they met my sister and I – walking down the sidewalk and told us they had just finished searching our porch for a gun.

Then there's the time I kept telling one of my nephews, "stay away from that housing complex, I dreamed you got into big trouble there. A few weeks later, he was facing 30 years in prison for attempted manslaughter for shooting a guy in retaliation as a result of the guy attacking him. They just don't listen!

Now, when I dream, some of my family members will tell me, ""when you dream about some numbers, let me know. I smile and say okay. I did share some numbers I dreamed about with a cousin (oops, my bad) and he won **$500** (he gave me $25 to put in church and I took it too – the offering basket didn't know it was from the lotto).

NOTE: I am not advocating the lottery because *"The blessing of the LORD brings wealth, and he adds no trouble to it."* **The life course or "paths" of God-fearing and the righteous are "made smooth" and directed by God (Proverbs 3:5-6; 16:1-3; and the fear of the Lord and humility bring wealth and honour (Proverbs 22:4).**

On the real side though, it was through dreams and visions that God called me into the ministry and I now see the value of dreams and visions. *"And it shall come to pass afterward, that I will pour out my spirit upon all flesh; and your sons and your daughters shall prophesy, your old men shall dream dreams, your young men shall see visions". Joel 2:28*

ONLY THE STRONG SURVIVE

While engaging in a telephone conversation one day with Rev. Lana Williams, an old friend, she asked me, "So when are you going to write that book?" (Lana had personal knowledge of some of my dark days). I said to her, I have started writing but I do not know if I can write about those dark places without hurting other people. She said to me, "There is a way to do it without all the ugly details." You know what Lana, you were absolutely right so here goes!

I think I know now why some people often defined me as "arrogant, militant, and she wears black." I suddenly realize that people were defining me as that person because they didn't really know me or understand that some of those characteristics were coming from – a place of early racism and inequality.

I often heard one of my cousins quote the words of a popular song, **"Only the Strong Survive" (by Jerry Butler),** but until I went through my valleys and ultimately developed a deeper and more meaningful relationship with Christ, those words were just resounding rhetoric. I have always had a strong determination to succeed and I wanted desperately to "be somebody". I wanted my life to count for something. I did not want to wind up on welfare with a house full of kids nor did I want to become a statistic – a young Black woman down on her luck story. I also wanted to prove the naysayers (in my hometown) wrong, who said I would never "finish school and would wind up with a house full of babies". I had dreams and I was determined to fulfill my *mother's* dreams for me! I was going places! I was going to college, get a good job and live the American Dream!

Growing up in small town Union Springs, Alabama (USA) had its perks but it also had its disadvantages. Growing up Black in the segregated South was to say the least, daunting! We were expected to adapt to the norm – which said - you are tolerated so don't make waves. Accept the fact that you will live in your neighborhoods across the railroad tracks, in the Bottom, or the Grove – but don't even *think* about going to *our* schools or living in our section of town!

Life was tough but at the time, we didn't really know how tough until we were subjected to blatant racism that showed us we were held to a different standard; a standard that said, you can't enter the front door of our eating establishments, you can't attend the "white" school that was obviously superior to the Black designated schools, you can't sit in the front of the bus, and you can only use the facilities designated for "Coloreds".

Life seemed to be simpler then, but by the time I became of school age, and started to ask questions of why I was treated differently, life became *really* complicated. Those complications helped to shape me into who I became – an inquisitive young girl who loved to read, go to school, and travel with my mother.

MoDear always seemed to be working harder and harder to try to give her family a good life and by the time I was old enough to enter first grade, I knew "**my world**" was different from that of the little white girls and boys living in our town!

During my first year in school, I could only attend school on a rotational basis (we did not have enough classrooms to accommodate all the children who were entering first grade), so one group had to attend from 8am to 12pm, while the other group attended from 12pm to 4pm. So what happens when a first grader forgets the rotational schedule? You guessed it – I missed out on school those days I was confused! It is worth mentioning here that I attended school during my fourth, fifth and sixth grades, in church buildings. Needless to say though, I loved school and didn't mind that I had to walk to school in all kinds of weather.

It's no wonder I am sometimes very saddened *now* when I see *our* children not going to school and not doing their very best. Blacks didn't even have access to the public library so every nickel or dime I came across, off to the store I went to buy books. I lived in USA until age 15 but never entered the library until 2007 when I returned there to live. I did not have adequate books, but I was able to finish high school and become very successful in my chosen occupational fields.

During 1960-1961, the teachers in USA had become increasingly disillusioned and were fed up with their low wages and inferior accommodations in the Bullock County School System. As a result of those circumstances, they decided to go on strike. MoDear always wanted us to go to school so she decided to let me move to Chicago to live with my sister Rosemary so that I would not miss school.

Chicago was a different animal! I was like a "duck out of water". There were high-rise buildings everywhere and they all looked alike to me. I remember riding my bike around the corner one day and wouldn't you know I was lost one street over from my house? Then when I started to school, I was as green as they came! I was so lost, I was in the basement looking for the fourth floor! Dumb huh? I had never been in a 4th floor building before – how was I to know how to get to Room 425? Well not to worry, a young man came to my rescue and decided he would be my personal guide until I could find my classes on my own! Can somebody say **BLESSED?**

I still loved school but now instead of having 15 students in the classroom I had left in USA, there were at least 25 students in my Chicago classrooms. I went from attending a segregated school in Alabama with caring and committed teachers to a very large semi-integrated school with some mediocre (collecting a paycheck) teachers.

However, I did not let that deter me and I still worked hard. Even though school was more of a challenge, I still managed to graduate with a decent grade point average. I had always dreamed of going into the military after high school but as fate would have it, I did not pass the entry exam and there went my dream of a military career (not to mention I was discouraged with the rhetoric, "a woman has no business in the military with all those men)."

I gave up way too soon – should've taken the exam again (racist 60's though). I still had dreams of going to college but I did not know anything about scholarships or grants and those counselors sure didn't volunteer any information.

You see, that's the difference of being in Chicago and being in USA where many of my former classmates in USA, went on to college – some of them on scholarships. You need a backup plan!

Yes, I know now what it says in **Jeremiah 29:11** but who knew then: *"For I know the thoughts that I think toward you, saith the* **Lord**, *thoughts of peace, and not of evil, to give you an expected end."*

If you're not going to school you know a job comes next right? Never had a job before so possibilities were limited. However, a neighbor/friend Ms. Mary, one door over, worked at a toy factory and informed me that they were indeed hiring! The HR Director informed me that she only had an opening for a Dictaphone operator – to which I replied, I know how to use a Dictaphone. After she couldn't dissuade me, I was hired as an Assembler on a Conveyor Belt Line (from Dictaphone Operator to putting pegs in square holes). Oh well, segregated South in the Midwest (or up North).

Working at that factory was a jungle. Craziness to the nth degree. Riding down that conveyor belt when I got behind trying to insert my parts into a box of road-racing sets. Then as fate would have it while working at that factory - along comes that proverbial tall, dark and handsome young man who I thought was my "knight in shining armor". He had come to rescue me, to make my dreams come true, to give me a life full of adventure. We would conquer the world together!

After we were married, I used to tell him, "the two of us will go places, we might not ever be rich but if we just hold on to each other, we will be okay". He agreed, often telling me, "with your brains and my hustle, we will make it."

However, to my dismay, this man-child would soon turn out to be just the opposite of those dreams we had so excitedly discussed, anticipated and desired.

Because we were much too young (I was 19 he was 21), to be married, we were soon swallowed up by his insecurity and my lack of judgment of what a good husband should be. The trouble started out of nowhere – or so I thought! I never knew that past family dynamics could influence a relationship.

Way too many episodes of drama to go into, that contributed to the demise of the marriage but just remember this – ladies, get to know him (especially the relationship he has with his siblings and parents). But of course that's another story!

As I look back remembering those years, I can only thank God that *He* did not let go of my hand. There were times when *I* almost let go but something deep inside me, spoke to me and admonished me to **"Get up and get out of there Jenny."** I now know that it was the Spirit of God *lifting* me up and the spirit of my praying mother *lifting* me up to Him.

I think that if I had stayed a moment longer, I would not have survived physically or mentally. I was on the brink! I was headed to a place of no return – on a fast roller coaster ride to God only knows where. However, God in His infinite wisdom lifted me just in the nick of time – His time.

How readily I can identify with those women in the Bible (Leah, Dinah and Hagar) who were battered, lonely and not valued as women. They did not have a voice of reason or a father to validate them with nurturing love.

Sometimes I found myself wishing I had brothers like Leah who would avenge me. I wanted someone bigger and stronger than me to come to my rescue – to take that bully down!

Even though I believed in God, there were times when I thought even *He* had abandoned me. Little did I know however that He was preparing me for something I could not see right then.

Now years later I find myself remembering that man-child with compassion and forgiveness and yes, even love. I can even talk to him with civility because God has purged me from the hurt, from the pain, the bitterness and anger.

You see, I now know that somewhere deep inside that man-child is a man who wants to emerge to become a loving, caring human being but he's afraid to let others know that he *too* is fragile and needs to be validated by God.

Like too many women – whether like the fictional character **Miss Celie from Alice Walker's "The Color Purple"** or the woman next door, we can all attest to the fact that if it had not been for the Lord on our side, where would we be? Can I get an Amen somebody?

While I do not go back to that dark place of physical and mental abuse, there is a lot to be said about the abuse I wreak on my own life by trying to find love in all the wrong places.

I am constantly reminding myself that I am not that little girl from USA who misses the daddy she lived with but never *really* knew; I am not that little frightened girl from USA who saw her mother trying to rise above her meager circumstances by being the major provider for her children; I am not that little girl who wanted a man to love her unconditionally. I am not that little girl who desperately longed to be held, understood and valued as a woman.

Moving from that place of too many sad memories and needing to give my teen-aged son, a chance at life, away from the "inner city", we moved down south. Being in a large urban city for many years had taken me to another dimension and my tolerance for complacency was short-lived.

I couldn't for the life of me understand why some folks in this small town, didn't demand the respect they so deserved.

I saw them being undervalued in the workplace - spoken to in a condescending manner and I was appalled. This is a different place! What have I done?! I am not prepared for this Lord! I want to go back to the City. I was so distraught, I made a telephone call to my old boss and he encouraged me to come on back to Chicago and a job would be created for me.

In the meantime, my son is in love with the freedom of FWB and tells me in no uncertain terms, "I don't want to go back Mom." Of course my motherly instincts kick in and I agree we're here now – things will work out alright. **"Only the strong survive."**

Despite having many years of job experience, and a college degree, it was hard for me to find a job of substance. Collecting unemployment from Chicago's system was more than a minimum waged job here in FWB and needless to say, this was not an incentive for me to want to give up my unemployment benefits.

Everywhere I went, I was told, "you're over-qualified". My question was, how can a person who needs a job, be overqualified? I just wanted to work and take care of myself and my son. The largest employer here in FWB, the Air Force, was undergoing a class-action suit for discriminating against Blacks, so that was not an option at the time.

In the meantime, I finally landed a part-time job in Retail Customer Service and did that for a few months until God found favor on me by placing a nice young lady from church (Mrs. Della Primous Rhodes) in my path. Della worked for the City of FWB and she told me about an opening in the Community Development Block Grant (CDBG) department.

I applied, and was hired as a secretary. It was while working in this program that I earned the moniker, "she wears black". Let me help you understand, yes I did wear a lot of black, but that was the code name for "she is a Black Power agitator!"

Yes, discrimination was still alive and well.

However, I wound up working for a really nice guy named Bill (Director of the program), who gave me opportunities to excel and move up. Upon Bill's moving to another city, he recommended me for his position. His decision was challenged from one of the City Councilmen with the question - "can she handle the job" **(while looking me squarely in the face).**

When Bill answered, "sure, she tells me what to do." I thought I had died and gone to heaven. After that great guy left, and I moved up to managing the CDBG Department, I found out that with new-found opportunities, comes new challenges and new fights.

Almost every decision I made - on how and where to spend funds, I was told, "you can't do that". Well for those of you who know me, know that I am not easily dismissed. I would pull out my copy of the Code of Federal Regulations and say, **"show it to me".**

Of course, I already knew it was just a ploy to keep us from doing what needed to be done to better our community. (one of the financial staff persons at that time always referred to the program as a "giveaway program").

As emphasized in Esther 4, (and as Pastor Thigpen has reminded me on occasion), that I was chosen for that position "for such a time as this" because our community was in dire need of revitalization.

With much prayer and putting my foot down, these changes were made under the direction of myself and my most capable co-worker, Mrs. Mary Cox (I could not have performed my job as effectively without her - she was awesome). But God!

Mary & Jenny were the BGR Team. We worked very hard to gain the trust of residents in the community and to this day, people still talk about CDBG (mostly positive but I'm sure we had "naysayers" as well but we were on a God-assigned mission). Fast-forward! Oh! Oh! Did I hear somebody ask, five months down the road, "Will you marry me?" Yes, I will! Whew! My head is spinning from the whirlwind courtship.

On with the story. Living through years of misunderstandings, losing some of my self-assuredness, losing too much of myself – succumbing to a world of the mundane. Nooo! Not again. I do not think I can survive this one God. Irreconcilable differences soon leads me to abandon yet another marriage. Lord, will I ever get it right? God I thought you loved me! *"Jenny my child, I will not put more on you than you can bear."* But God, it sure does hurt.

Friends, family and loved ones rallied around me and again, God shows up as only He can. Wouldn't you know, once is not enough and twice we try to make a go of the marriage. Again, I find it necessary to forgive and to actually feel the pain of a man who keeps too much of himself bottled up inside. Honey, when are you going to let it go and let God birth in you that loving and giving spirit that lurks just below the surface? I know a **MAN** who can love you like no one else can. **HE** can bring you into a brand new awareness of who He wants you to be.

Too much pain! Too much mistrust! There is no way I can go through this again. God will you be upset with me if I leave? Thank you God for lifting me up. ***"Lord take care of my child."* MoDear, I hear you praying for me in the Spirit. I can feel you lifting me up too!**

I am paralyzed with depression and I do not want to move from the couch. I go to work but I am just an empty shell. I show up at church and was asked one Sunday – by one of the associate ministers, "so how you doing this morning." When I responded, 'I am depressed', he admonishes me with "Christians don't get depressed." So if you don't want to know how I feel, why did you ask? Thank God for deliverance! We know that Christians indeed do get depressed but it's a place we don't linger!

I know that "**faith comes by hearing**" because it was late one night while listening to the gospel being preached on a gospel TV station, with Donnie McClurkin and BeBe Winans singing *"Stand,"* that my faith is strengthened. What a powerful testimony of that song! To this day, I love that song and I become so emotional, listening to it.

Many nights I stay up all night tossing and turning unable to sleep. I keep hearing those voices! *Please leave me alone!* I keep having those visions. *Please, just go away and leave me alone! I just want to sleep!*

How long will I have to endure this dark cloud lurking over me – tossing me into a deep abyss? I can't take the pain! Not even going to church can help the uncertainty I'm feeling. The uncertainty of not knowing where I fit into the whole scheme of things as relates to my life in general, the uncertainty of feeling like a complete failure when it comes to marriage.

Here comes one of those cosmic visions again! I am looking into a mirror with faces flashing in front of me and I hear a distinctive voice saying. *"Virginia, I want you to preach to my sons, and to my grandsons." (I knew this was serious because during this time, everyone referred to me as Jenny).*

Another space, another time. I'm in church (Beulah First Baptist – FWB), when I try to literally shove the words of **Isaiah 61:1-3,** back into my mouth.

"The Spirit of the Lord GOD is upon me; because the LORD hath anointed me to preach good tidings unto the meek; he hath sent me to bind up the brokenhearted, to proclaim liberty to the captives, and the opening of the prison to them that are bound).

God, I know you are not talking to me. I do not want to be a preacher. Lord, can't you find somebody else? Okay God, if I must, but I'm warning you, I don't like it! Through many unusual dreams, visions and promptings from the Holy Spirit, I finally give in to the call of God's voice. *Yes God – I will preach your Word.*

Fast-forward. After moving to Atlanta after things didn't work out in the relationship, I feel it's time to share my **CALL** with my pastor at my new church. He counsels with me and starts to prepare me by doing preliminary work and studying; getting me prepared for ministerial training. I am in training about 18 months and it is finally time for me to be licensed and on Sunday, December 16, 2001, I am licensed to become a gospel preacher! Praise be to God for His mighty acts!

Ministry is great and I enjoy and love preaching and teaching the Word! However, wouldn't you know that **Gypsy** spirit is rising again! I've been in contact with my sister Rosemary and I decide to move back to Chicago to be with her after the loss of her long-time friend Pete. I apply for and receive a job offer with a local Federal Agency.

I return to my former church and man do I have the time of my life – working with the youth, teaching and preaching! God is so good! I love being back in my old neighborhood – same building I grew up in and making a difference on the block!

It is during this time that I start a not-for-profit organization (Mirror of Dreams Workshop, Inc.) to work with young people. My vision has come into fruition (*"**Virginia, I want you to preach to my sons, and to my grandsons).**"*

I lived in Chicago for three years (2002-2004). Did you not know that subtle racism is still alive and well even in the big city?

I witnessed discrimination from one manager (he dismissed one guy, gave two of us Black employees satisfactory performance ratings (no way I was satisfied with getting a less than excellent rating – as I received in all my former Federal jobs). Time for me to be moving on. "All my life, I had to fight." **(Sophia from the Color Purple).**

Back to Atlanta I go to my former job! I am a blessed Child of the King! I told you I am not arrogant! It is that self-confidence shining through.

Confidence in knowing that there is a God that cares about me; confidence in knowing that I am somebody in Him! He knows my name, He knows my pain and He knows the *real* me. He is waiting to nurture that little girl from USA who can tell you about being strong. Not In my might but strong in the power of His might. I now know that I do not need a man to validate me!

There is still that little girl from USA peering from behind those shutters but this time she knows without a shadow of a doubt, that *only the strong survive!* Surviving to be able to think about retirement. It is 2006 and *I've* decided that I loved being in Chicago so much that I want to retire and move back - had already talked to my Pastor about working at the church. Notice I said, *I* decided to retire. Wouldn't you know, God had other plans for my life!

I get a call from Ft. Walton Beach – my husband had just suffered a major stroke! We were still married but living apart. Ok – I'll be there in a short while. I arrive and find that even though he did not suffer any permanent damage to limbs, he is going to need help rehabilitating and should not be living alone.

We move him to Atlanta where he remains with me for a year until I retire in 2007. He wanted a change of scenery from FWB and he didn't want to live in Atlanta. We decided to move to USA. I thought I would be able to adjust to living again in small town USA – but whew! I try very hard but find it is zapping my energy, spirit and soul! After four years I just can't do it any longer!

In order to help you understand my heart and spirit a little better, allow me to share this: I've often joked with my friends and family about my being a gypsy.

As you may know, "gypsies are a race of nomads who early on - typically carried their belongings in covered wagons and pitched tents wherever they stopped. It has been said that for them, traveling is not a pastime or leisure activity, but a way of life. In fact, a common belief of the latter part of the nineteenth century suggested that the inclination to travel, called "wanderlust," was a product of genetic determinants."

I'm not suggesting that I have an inclination to pitch a tent nor do I have a lack of religious preference as did most gypsies early on, but I do understand and identify with the nomadic spirit of the gypsy lifestyle.

While watching an old episode of the western, Bonanza, on *May 11, 2009*, I understand even more my spirit of wandering. The episode featured a young gypsy girl accused by her people of being a witch (simply because her spirit is different and non-traditional).

There was something very profound that this young woman verbalized in that episode: *"I've often looked at fish swimming around in the stream; I've looked in their eyes, wanting to become one of them."* However, she was held captive by so many demons from her past she could not be free to swim.

At that instant, I connected with that young gypsy girl (albeit it was only a fictional show). You see, years ago, I started signing my name *Freedom is my signature,* with a depiction of a bird whenever I sent greeting cards to that special friend who always reminded me to love myself.

Just as that young woman identified with those fish, I found myself identifying with birds because they have no constraints. They spread their wings and fly! Some even soar. They have no limits – they decide in which direction to go next. I am sitting there on my deck listening to birds singing. There are so many different songs being sung at the same time that I can't distinguish them all. The irony of those birds singing remind me that there are so many songs I want to sing, so many lives to touch, so many messages to deliver that I don't want to remain in one place! I want to fly! I **NEED** to soar! The gypsy girl in me is awakened again -- *she* needs to be free! She is not at home right now because she keeps coming to roost in places where freedom is limited. Limited by a lack of non-communication and by communal disconnectedness. She misses the interaction of friends and family with whom she has a special bond – those who can make her laugh, encourage her to dance and who support her dreams!

You see it really hit me like a ton of bricks early one morning and literally brought me to tears. Tears because there is a revelatory truth - I have never really come to this place before where I recognize why I feel so closed in – never wanting to remain in one place for a very long period. There is an ever-present truth that reminds me of the pain I endured for so long.

I am especially reminded of that pain when I witness other Sistahs going through! I feel that if I don't flee this place, I will wither away and literally die! So what if I've been here and put down roots! *Pull up those roots and prepare to transplant them elsewhere – in more fertile ground. I know you would prefer to live in the "City" but circumstances circumvent those dreams right now! Girl, haven't you always learned how to adapt? Yea – you can make it – with God on your side and your ability to see the glass half-full! Now, pick yourself up and do what you gotta do!*

Moving back to FWB was not the panacea I envisioned nor was it my first choice but I seem to wear sacrifice well. *"Virginia my child, I will not put more on you than you can bear."*

So here I am! Settled into an all too familiar place but not without disappointments. Disappointment in ministry and disappointment in so many things that are important to that not so little girl from USA. *"Lord do it for me."* God whatever you do, let it be to your glory and for the up-building of your kingdom!*

"YOU MEAN YOU WROTE THAT?"

MoDear was very impressed with my writing and she once expressed to me (upon reading some poetry and short stories I had written), **"you mean you wrote that?"**

READING AND WRITING HAS ALWAYS BEEN MY PASSION AND A SOURCE OF ESCAPE. THE FOLLOWING ARE JUST A SMALL SAMPLING OF MY WRITINGS:

JUXTAPOSITION - 6 June 2000 - 3:30 a.m.

I'm singing a song but there's no melody --- there's a void. I'm writing a poem but the words don't rhyme --- there's a void. My soul is longing for love but there is no one --- there's a void. You say *you* love me but you don't want commitment --- there's a void. I trusted you with my heart but you walked on it like shattered eggshells there's a void. My tears are flowing but I can't taste them --- there's a void. My eyes are like mirrors but there is no reflection --- there's a void. I'm seeking for answers but I am afraid to accept the truth --- there's a void. I dream in color but my life reflects dark shadows – there's a void. I have hope but I sometimes let naysayers influence my decisions --- there's a void. I know I have a purpose but I sometimes walk aimlessly --- there's a void. There's a Void! There's A Void! There's A Void!

AFRICA'S EXODUS - February 1992

The book of Exodus, tells of a people's bitter struggle to gain their freedom from pharaoh. It also tells how these people endured much in their determination to escape a fate worse than death. In this poem, Africa's Exodus, it relates the saga of our ancestors who were snatched from their native country and parallels the similarities Black people had with those of the people of Israel.

And when she was yet in her maidenhood, they swooped down upon her like a vulture – devouring her. They ripped open her swollen belly and trampled upon her

Young like a mighty crushing wall, crumpling her into nothingness. I heard her hollow cries, echoing throughout the mystical pyramids and I remembered.

I looked through the tainted telescope of time and my mind was flooded with the many injustices she was made to suffer. Africa, oh Africa, your sons and daughters cry out.
Exodus! Exodus!

And the Lord God spoke unto Moses, "go unto Pharaoh, and say unto him, thus saith the Lord, Let my people go, that they may serve me."

They gathered her young together upon the auction block, Their backs were beaten into raw and festering sores.

"And Moses said, we will go with our young and with our old, with our sons and with our daughters with our flocks and with our herds will we go,

For we must hold a feast unto the Lord".
Africa, oh Africa, your sons and daughters await you.
Exodus! Exodus!

When they put her sons and daughters in chains,
Their pride was crushed; spirits bruised, minds shackled,
Left to grovel in the dust for scraps like worthless dogs.

But the Lord God said unto Moses, "Behold, I will rain manna from heaven for you, and the people shall go out and gather a certain rate every day

That I may prove them, whether they will walk in my law or no."
"And thou shalt observe the feast of weeks of the first fruits of wheat harvest and the feast of ingathering at the year's end. Then saith he unto his disciples,

"The harvest is plenteous, but the laborers are few".
Africa, oh Africa, your sons and daughters love you.
Exodus! Exodus!

Today my voice cries out to the sons and daughters,
Arise oh ye great nation! "Remember now the days of thy youth!"
Claim your heritage and your rich legacy!

Africa, oh Africa, your sons and daughters are proud of you.
We thank God for you and we stand true to you, our native land.
Africa, oh Africa, your sons and daughters are reborn to you!
Exodus! Exodus!

SPECTRUM

4/18/2002 - 5:32 p.m.

While walking in downtown Chicago on a beautiful

Spring day - I encounter ...

Smiling faces, scowling faces, happy faces, depressed faces, hopeful
faces, doubtful faces.

I don't give a flying flip about *nothing* faces.

Talking to yourself and beating yourself down faces;

Going nowhere faces. In my mind I'm thinking

'There's nothing like the downtown streets of Chicago',

As I walk briskly amongst those spectrum of faces.

For a fleeting moment my soul looks deeply into each face,

Beholding the beauty as it tries desperately to surface.

Trying not to bear witness to the pain as it takes over.

Beauty still surrounds me however as I listen to echoing sounds

Of cultural happenings just around the corner and as I anticipate
seeing a face that will spark

A memory of a long ago place.
I'm almost back at my office – there it is!

A face getting off the elevator – an old high school face,

Face of success! Hello so how've you been?

"So you're an attorney now? How awesome!"
Nothing like downtown Chicago on a balmy spring afternoon

As the wind and the sun gently caresses all those faces!

~~~~~~~~~~~

TO A YOUNG SISTAH

17 SEPT 1997 - 1:00 A.M.

Come here my young Sistah and let me embrace your innocence
before you become a woman too soon. Let me embrace you so you
can laugh and live your magical dreams;

To fling rainbow-colored bubbles in the wind, to jump Double-
Dutch with your Whimsical rope while singing along to the lyrics of
your favorite song. Come my young Sistah and let me tell you about
that smooth talking,

"What's your name baby girl" Brotha, who wants to whisper sweet
nothings in your ear,

Who wants to rob you of your girlhood dreams of becoming a
lawyer, a doctor, or an Astronaut, oh yes, you can even become
president if you want to. *Hello!*

Come my young Sistah and let me teach you lessons about your rich
ancestry

That has woven us together in strong determination, and never giving up!

Let me tell you about how it cost somebody something for you to be free!

Of what it means to be truly yourself, of what it means to know your purpose!

Of how you can do all things through Christ who strengthens you! And of how you can rise to any occasion!

Come my young Sistah and let me be your friend, Your mentor, your teacher, so you will know how to love yourself, how to hug yourself,

How to trust your instincts, how to claim success, how to be proud of *you*!

Cause baby you are *somebody* and yes, you are also beautiful.

And when you *really* find your place inside yourself, and claim your niche in the world,

Come let me introduce you to kings and queens,

To the great Pyramids of Africa, to the Euphrates *and* the Nile.

But in the meantime, don't forget to look in the mirror,

Because the image you see there is me --

Looking back at you with pride and encouragement.

Come along my young Sistah, for the journey begins now!

Take that first step, but don't walk too fast toward womanhood,

Because you still have time to enjoy laughter that comes with being young.

Come my young Sistah and let me embrace you, so your innocence will be revered!

YOU DON'T KNOW ME

December 31, 2013 – 12:15 p.m.

If you don't know my story, my struggles, my fears and my heartbreaks, then you don't know me. You can't look at me *now* and think you know me based on what you perceive. Your definition of me doesn't *even* scratch the surface of what I have been through.

If you don't know the pain and humiliation I have been through due to physical, and emotional abuse then you don't know me.

If you don't know how patiently I waited for the pain, the hurtful words, the betrayal, and the emptiness to be over, then you don't know me.

Therefore, before you define me again, think about *who* you see and who you think you know, because you don't *really* know me!

FOR US ALL - December 05, 2002

A Tribute In Memory Of MoDear's Birthday

As MoDear wove beautiful threads together to make hats, scarves, and Afghans,

Let us remember the beautiful array of colors she wove together

In our lives in the form of Loving, caring, sharing, and faithfulness.

Let each color represent the Uniqueness of each of her offspring and pray that we

Never forget the Beauty of each thread that Intertwine our lives today because of her!

YOU ARE THE SONSHINE OF MY LIFE

On February 23, 1967, a beautiful baby boy was born to that little Alabama girl! He was the cutest baby! Grew by leaps and bounds and before long, was a tall, lanky, handsome young man! Terence –aka- Tiger was a privileged kid (everybody spoiled him rotten).

He was such a joy to watch – enjoying his cousins and wrapping his Big Mama around his little finger. My Sister, Big Mama was so attached to him, and he to her that he never wanted to go home. When I remember his first steps, his birthday parties and his school days, it's like I am transported back in time! He was/is truly the 'sonshine of my life."

Watching him grow up trying to figure out where he fit in, was sometimes very frightening for me. I wondered, am I being too strict, too lenient or what? A friend once told me I was too strict because he was actually put on punishment for a small infraction. So you can see I was often torn wondering if maybe I was too strict. But you know what, that same friend's grandson wound up in prison and it was confirmed – no I'm not too strict.

Tiger's teenaged years growing up in FWB were hopefully some of his fondest memories because I often told myself, "It was for him that we wound up in FWB. Once he graduated high school, he went away to a two-year community college on a basketball scholarship. I firmly suggested he join the Reserves to earn some spending money while he was away in school (one weekend a month). **NOTE:** He was given two choices (1) College or (2) Military; he emphatically told me, "The military is not for me"!

After graduation, who shocks me by proclaiming "I'm going active duty into the Army! Say what! I thought you didn't like the military! I was crushed! I wanted him to finish another two years of school. Oh well, all is not lost. After thirteen years of active duty (getting married in between time, having two beautiful sons – Jayson and Dominique) serving for seven years of reserve duty, seven years as a Wichita police officer and currently working as a police officer with the City of FWB, I believe he has found his niche.

I must say, there has never been a prouder mother of her child than I am of my "Tiger"

TO GOD BE THE GLORY FOR THE VILLAGE

PROGRESSION

ELEMENTARY SCHOOL

HIGH SCHOOL

ARMY LIFE

WE ARE FAMILY

CLARENCE & JULIA HALL FAMILY TREE

ELLA RUTH	LILLIAN	ROSEMARY	VIRGINIA
Alfred	Anthony	Jerry	Terence
Beverly	Patricia	Alonza	
Cynthia	Angela	Maurice	
Tonya	Sandy	Mary	
Mangano	Chauncey	Mable	
Darryl	Pleshette	Theresa	

FEBRUARY 23, 2019

BAHAMAS CRUISE ABOARD THE CARNIVAL

Celebrating Tiger's Birthday

Left: Jenny, Ella, Beverly, Cynthia

Right: Tonya, Jennefir, Dianne, Azalea

MY BEAUTIFUL SISTER ROSEMARY HALL-HUGHES

The Bible tells us in Isaiah 40:29-31, that "God strengthens the weary and gives vitality to those worn down by age and care. Young people will get tired; strong young men will stumble and fall. But those who trust in the Lord will regain their strength. They will soar on wings as eagles. They will run and won't give out of breath. They will walk and not get tired, and will never faint."

Rosemary was worn, she stumbled, she was often weary but she stayed in the race for the long haul. She is now soaring like an eagle because God gave her the strength she needed to endure the struggle and now she has entered into eternal rest where she will never have to worry about starting or finishing a race. My sister Rosemary was a runner when she was in school and I am sure that when she was preparing for a race, she had to go through training and she had to set goals for herself in order to win a race.

Well, life is pretty much like a race. We have to prepare ourselves by relying on the true and living God and we must believe that every Word he says is true. In the end, we win some and we lose some but with God we are never losers!

All of us who knew Rosemary, know that she was a very fierce competitor – not only in racing, but in other activities such as Bid Whist, Spades, etc. If you just happened to be her partner – forget about ever getting the chance to bid – because if you said a "SIX NO" – she was going to say a seven – and we are still trying to figure out how she so often won (without cheating).

I am reminded of a story that my sister Ruth shared with us about an incident that happened when they were young – hanging out at the club. A fight broke out, the police were called and witnesses stepped up to give their testimony. Rose stepped up, gave her version of the incident and the police officer just happened to look down at her feet. He pushed her to the side and told her – "I know you didn't see anything because you were running so fast, you lost your shoes."

Even though Rosemary was an excellent runner, the race she ran best was the one she completed on June 24, 2013. God helped her to "lay aside every weight". Abandoning everything that could hold her back". She called on the name of Jesus and He heard and pitted her every groan. We may not understand the course she chose to run, but we need to remember why we are running, and that we should continually train for the race to meet our Savior just as Rosemary did.

My advice to you today is: There is never a bad time to begin preparing for the race. God is waiting to greet you at the finish line, so put on your running shoes and start running as if your life depends on it – because it does!

GALLERY

Top Left to Right: Tiger, MoDear, Tiger & MoDear
Bottom Left to Right: MoDear, Tiger, Tiger & Me

(MY HANDSOME SONS)

Mom & Marcus   **Mom & Terence**

Terence & Jennefir

Stacey & Marcus

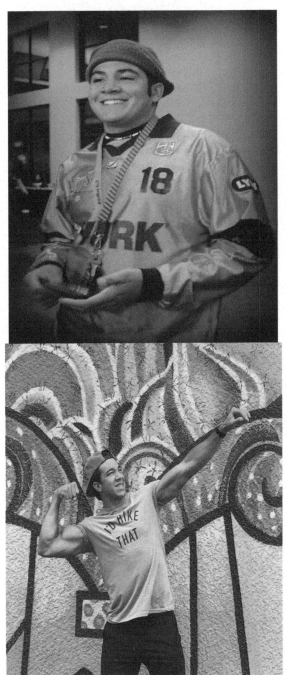

Grandsons - Dominique & Jayson

Grandson, Marcus

My Beautiful Granddaughter, Taylor

Sister, Ella & Niece, CJ

Nieces – Tonya, Meoka, Diane (Lady Di), BJ
"Mikki", You Did That Thang Girl!
Stepped outta that comfort zone and just grabbed that Master's Degree!
Look at all that Beauty (It's in the Genes Baby)

Hima, Bonnie, Rosemary, Shaun
Nothing Like Family Love & Ties

Captain Darryl
My Inspirational Conversationalist

"BJ"
Gifted Beyond Measure

Adopted Daughter, Karen
I am always lifting you up daughter (I love your creativity)!

Queen Bonnie
You Rock From The Inside Out!

Alonza a-k-a "SILK"
"When God gets through with you, you shall come forth as pure gold."

The Other "Blues Brothers"
'Tiger' – "Unk" – "Tree"
Not Only Cousins But Brothers Bonding

Marcus & Terence
Brothers Extraordinare

TOP: Hubby - James; Sister – Betty
BOTTOM LEFT (FRONT) – Pleshette, Harold, Lilliam, Pat
BOTTOM (REAR) – Chauncey, Angela, Sandy, Tony

Son, Laffie

Daughter, Jasamine

MY BEAUTIFUL, CAPTIVATING & INTELLIGENT GOD-DAUGHTERS

April & Latoya

Amber

WHEN YOU FEEL THE RHYTHM – JUST DANCE

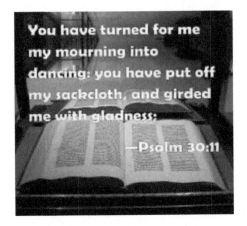

Tiffany Thornton-Andrews (Dance Like David Danced)

SERVING GOD

Y'all Better Get Right With God

MoDear would often tell us, "Y'all better get right with God." When we were young, MoDear instilled in us, the importance of being "saved" and attending church on a regular basis. When she wasn't working, she took us to church and when she was working, we found ourselves attending church in our neighborhood – by ourselves.

However, when we became of age and having moved out on our own, we didn't always carry on that tradition of attending church and Sunday School. We would get so tired of hearing that same old tune – **"y'all better get right with God."** Some of <u>you</u> know what I'm talking about – you've "been there, done that."

Wouldn't you know that Scripture rings true when it says, in **Proverbs 22:6 when it says: "Train up a child in the way he should go, and when he is old he will not depart from it." (KJV)** It took me going through those dark valleys I talked about earlier and realizing that what I needed, I could not find anywhere but in the Word of God and through a personal relationship with Father/Son/Holy Spirit. I often think how different my life would've been if I had developed a deeper relationship with God earlier in my life. I would be the first to admit however, that just being "saved" was not enough. I was still doing things contrary to the Word of God and just living life to **"my fullest"**. But when I truly, truly, came into the knowledge of "grace, mercy and eternal life, my life changed and it has never been the same.

Those things that previously upset me, has now become sources of laughter. "They were not/and are not that serious. I can still hear MoDear telling me, "you better get right with God" and I can truly say, I wouldn't have it any other way!

While attending worship services one Sunday, in USA, my family participated in the service by singing one of our favorite songs. Everyone was into the service -- clapping, rocking and raising a Hallelujah hand into the air! MoDear was there having herself a grand ole time! (I always carried a writing tablet and a black marker with me to church so I could tell her what was going on). When I tell you that the Holy Spirit works miracles, you best believe me, because after service was over, MoDear said to those in the group, ***"Chillun, I didn't know y'all could sing like that".*** Everybody was like whoa! She heard music that day. It was so amazing to see someone totally deaf, get carried away in the Spirit.

NO FEAR

2 Timothy 1:7 reminds us that "For God hath not given us the spirit of fear; but of power, and of love, and of a sound mind". In this scripture, Paul reminds Timothy that the spirit of fear intends to keep us from fulfilling the destiny that God has on our lives; from living joyful, spirit- led lives where we show love to others as a result of the love God pours into our lives.

God has given us sound minds which means that our thoughts can be shielded from the lies of the devil (those crazy thoughts that try to overtake our minds). However, when we come into the knowledge of who God is, all we have to do is rely on His Word and the Holy Spirit to keep us intact.

I often reflect on the times I lived in Chicago and Atlanta – riding public transportation to work. From day-to-day, I never knew what kind of drama I would encounter. I can distinctly remember some of those instances:

- A young woman obviously under the influence of drugs, sat just behind me – nodding out and falling asleep. A Voice kept telling me to turn around and say something to her; to which I kept arguing, I a'int saying **nothing** to that lady. Well, lo and behold I couldn't rest until I obeyed the Voice. Long story short – I said to her - my Sistah, wake yourself up – God loves you. I kept repeating it about three or four times and to my amazement, a guy was sitting in front of me holding a Bible and every time I said something, he would say AMEN (I never even noticed him before then – can somebody say Angel). I know that woman was tired of me, but I couldn't rest and I wouldn't let her rest. After a while she just burst into tears and told me, I'm not from around here. I told her, it doesn't matter where you live - you don't have to live like this, wake yourself up! I kept trying to console her and it was finally time for me to get off the train. I got up staggering like a drunken woman almost unable to walk – drained. Fear never entered my mind while I was ministering to her and I felt nothing but love for her even though I didn't know her. The Spirit will do that! **NO FEAR!**

- Then there's the time about four or five rowdy teenage boys got on the train – talking loud, using profanity and just being obnoxious. I was riding with my train buddy Esther and we kept looking at each other. After I couldn't take any more, I asked them, so why aren't you guys in school. They looked at me and at each other and immediately started to make excuses. They were blaming each other saying it was his fault – for talking them into ditching school. Of course they were in for an old-fashioned motherly lecture about the ills of skipping school and being disrespectful in public (no harsh words, just genuine concern). To my surprise, they didn't get ugly with me, just listened and said yes mam, when I told them I didn't want to ever see them on that train again cutting up. Esther told me I was "nuts" and she was shaking in her "boots". **NO FEAR**

- Another time I'm on the bus and a guy gets on without paying his fare. The bus driver just sits there – tells him, I'm not moving until you pay your fare. He sat there – didn't move that bus! Mind you, I worked from 2p.m.-10 p.m. while attending school before work - three hours a day. I was tired, fuming, hungry, and was not in any mood for nonsense. I turned around, tells this guy – 'you need to come up here and pay your fare because I am tired and if I can pay, you got to pay'. I stared him down and the bus did not move. He finally gets up, brings his crazy butt up there and drops his fare in the box. I was like, thank you; everybody on the bus cheering – I'm like why did I, a woman have to say something when the bus was full of men as well. **NO FEAR!**

NOTE: Even though I had no fear then (at least 17 years ago), times are different now and I would not confront people on public transportation being 75 years old (I can't fight).

Seriously, there are times when we still have to speak up when we see wrongdoing but we must use different methods. I am not advocating that anyone resort to tactics that put them in harm's way, because each individual's journey is differently ordained by God. However, serving God does pay off and in the end, our **FAITH** will win out over **FEAR!**

**Jenny's Initial Sermon: JESUS' BLOOD BRINGS NEW LIFE -
Scripture Reference: John 3:1-7**

Then Jesus said unto them, "There was a man of the Pharisees, named Nicodemus, a ruler of the Jews: The same came to Jesus by night, and said unto him, Rabbi, we know that thou art a teacher come from God: for no man can do these miracles that thou doest, except God be with him; Jesus answered and said unto him, Verily, verily, I say unto thee, Except a man be born again, he cannot see the kingdom of God. Nicodemus saith unto him, how can a man be born when he is old? Can he enter the second time into his mother's womb, and be born? Jesus answered, "Verily, verily, I say unto thee, except a man be born of water and *of* the Spirit, he cannot enter into the kingdom of God. That which is born of the flesh is flesh; and that which is born of the Spirit is spirit. Marvel not that I said unto thee, "Ye must be born again."

My mother, or "MoDear" as she was affectionately known, was a midwife. She delivered babies! I can distinctly remember her getting calls, sometimes very late at night or early morning. I can remember the ritual that MoDear went through as she prepared to go on her journey. First it was, *"get my bag child; where are my glasses; get me some underwear; give me my teeth; find my shoes; hurry up now, I got to go"!* And so the story goes. MoDear was a highly excitable woman and could be very dramatic. But now as I look back and I realize the awesomeness of an impending *new birth*, I fully understand why she became so excited. She was being faced with many uncertainties and risks.

I can imagine her asking herself as she prepared to make her delivery, *"Will I make it in time, will the baby or babies be all right, and will the mother be all right? Will I run into problems?"*

And there were risks -- sometimes of losing the baby and maybe even the mother -- there was just no telling. Those babies that my mother delivered were born in darkness, but their parents had high hopes and dreams that one day they would walk in the light and radiate in God's love. And just as those babies were destined for the light, Jesus came into the world to give light to those who He knew would wander in darkness. He was born so that we could be free and through that freedom, our purpose would be fulfilled.

I witnessed my mother's reverence and love for God that would later help sustain me in some of *my* darkest hours and had it not been for her guidance, her teachings and her never-ending faith, I would not have learned early on, how good God is. I would not have known that God is truly worthy to be praised and I would not know that there is victory in praising Him.

Let me briefly share with you a series of visions during my call into the ministry that shows a significant parallel between water and blood.

In one of my visions, my sisters Ella and Rosemary are walking alongside me, holding me up on each side. I am caught up in the Spirit, so weak I could not walk alone --staggering like a drunken woman. I kept telling them; *just get me to the water! Just get me to the water! Just get me to the water.*

I felt that if I could just get to the water, my strength would be renewed and everything would be all right. Oh you know how you have felt when you were thirsty on a very hot day and all your body wanted was a cool drink of water!

Can you remember the feeling you had after drinking that water – a feeling that nothing else could have satisfied you but that water? Let's reflect a moment as we look at the story of Jesus as He encountered the Samaritan woman at the well. Jesus was very tired because of His long journey on his way to Galilee. Jesus turned to this woman and said, please give me a drink. The woman was astonished because she knew that no Jew would ever have dealings with a Samaritan, so she replied, ***"How is it that you a Jew, is asking me a Samaritan for a drink?"*** Jesus said to the woman, "if you knew God's gift, and who it is who said to you, "Give me a drink', you would have asked him for living water, and he would have given it to you."

Jesus goes on to tell the woman that drinking the well water would not quench her thirst, but that "Whoever, drinks the living water that I will give him, will never thirst. The water that I will give him will be a spring of water inside him, welling up to eternal life." I just wanted to taste that living water!

Then there's the vision where I am lying in a pool of blood, and I'm frantically trying to stop the flow of blood – pushing it back into my side. One of my nephews, Mangano is leaning over me with a big smile on his face and he keeps repeating, "She's dying, she's dying". But I look up at him through feverish eyes and cry out, ***"I can't die yet, no I can't die yet, God still has something for me to do."***

Do you see the parallel here? The water and the blood -- both elements of a baby's birth and elements of Jesus' death? The blood representing new life and the water symbolic of cleansing and strength. Today I am able to tell you that Jesus is a Savior for those who need light in dark places, and to tell a dying world that He is waiting to give that living water to all who will freely accept it.

God has empowered me, through the blood of Jesus to bear witness to His birth, His death, His burial and His resurrection and as Isaiah 61:1-2 proclaims: "The Spirit of the Lord GOD is upon me; because the LORD hath anointed me to preach good tidings unto the meek; he hath sent me to bind up the brokenhearted, to proclaim liberty to the captives, and the opening of the prison to them that are bound; To proclaim the acceptable year of the LORD, and the day of vengeance of our God; to comfort all that mourn."

When you have been washed in the Blood of Jesus, you will feel compelled to proclaim liberty to those who are captives and preach good tidings to the meek. When you have been washed in His blood you will have power to witness to those who have no dreams; power to encourage those who lack vision; power to love others; and the power to forgive.

Sometimes we are not willing to accept Jesus' forgiveness and love because we feel that we must pay a debt that we owe Him. However, we must remember that we can never repay that debt. Jesus, the Son of the Living God, shed His precious blood to pay the infinite price for our countless sins. Now we are free to pursue a relationship with God that is motivated by gratitude and energized by the power of the Holy Spirit. Finally, just as my mother witnessed the awesomeness of delivering those newborn babies into the world years ago, we can now witness the awesomeness of Jesus the Christ as He gives us a new birth through His shed blood.

In **Revelation 21:6**, Jesus promises to give the thirsty, water as a gift -- perpetual water like a spring within – that waters forever and gives eternal life.

Are you thirsty? Do you want to drink from that perpetual well? Do you want to be washed in His precious blood? Will you let the blood of Jesus give you new life today? Are you willing to accept the free Gift?

IN THE MEANTIME: THEY ALSO GOT A STORY TO TELL

For years, other Sistah girlfriends and I have shared our stories of pain, suffering and despair. So, today my sistahs, you are being lifted up because I have become your voice -- to let the world know that we are more than conquerors through Jesus the Christ who loves us.

NOTE: This section of comments and reflections of the author and other women, are not meant to dehumanize our abusers but are meant to be transparent so our healing can begin for us, our daughters, our nieces, our aunts, and other women who have been abused. We must allow ourselves to confront, vent, question and ask why, so we can determine to forgive, once we establish a truthful dialogue. Come here girl and witness to how you made it over:

Sistah # 1: "He always told me how much he loved me; but how could he love me when he insisted on being condescending and belittling me -- telling me I would never amount to anything." How could he love me when he was selfish with his money, his car, his house, and his affections? You know what, one day I looked in the mirror and I saw a beautiful creature staring back at me. I saw that she was **"wonderfully and fearfully made."** She was made in the image of God and that's when I realized I was on to something -- there was no turning back. I no longer needed him to affirm me. I no longer needed him to validate me as a woman or as a person. I no longer needed him to take care of me. You see, God's love was radiating all around me, through me, around me, and it set me on a path to higher grounds; "makes me wanna holler" when I think of how much God loves me and all the beautiful blessings he has showered upon me. I am so glad God's prophecy is stronger than his because I did amount to **SOMEBODY!**

Sistah # 2: "When I was a young girl about 17, I was domestically abused by my much older boyfriend. One day he brought his other woman to the apartment we shared together. After being romantic with me, he goes into the other room and becomes involved with her. Then he comes out of the bedroom and forces me to make dinner for *them*. I was constantly being traumatized, brutalized, and threatened by this man. I can't count the number of times the police came to our apartment. I have to stop the pain. I'm trapped. I need to escape! One night he starts an argument – threatening to hurt me; half asleep, I grab a knife and plunge it into his body. No more pain for me or so I thought. Years later I am still a mess --- an alcoholic, trapped inside myself, knowing I killed him. I'm living in prison without bars. God please help me!"

Sistah # 3: "What man with any decency would push his naked wife out into an apartment hallway at 2:00 a.m. and close the door behind her? Did you say until death do us part, in sickness and in health? Can't you feel my pain? There's nothing healthy about you humiliating me! What happened to the sweet mild mannered guy you used to be? Did you let the cocaine possess you, did you let the bright lights blind you or are you under a generational curse? What happened?" Anyway, through God's grace, I forgive you. You don't have to be ashamed to look me in the eyes when we meet. I love you with the Love of God."

Sistah # 4: "I told him to leave me alone. I guess I just snapped." He always found a way to push my button. He was always fighting me. Seems like he would just sit around thinking of ways to make my life miserable. We had a house full of small children; life was hard. I remember leaving the house on several occasions to escape his physical abuse. Lord knows I was tired of running out in all that bad weather! I am at my wits end. I am tired of this fool! I got *his* gun out, shot his butt; ask me if he ever hit me again!"

Sistah # 5: "How come it's alright for him to go to boy's night out, but when I go to girl's night out, he comes looking for me? All is never fair in love and war. He made it a habit of trying to keep me behind closed doors I guess, so I would not run into him in the streets in his "mess". Girl, he was crazy! Asked me to pull my underwear off one time, so he could smell them -- wanted to see if I had been with another man! What was he thinking? I had never been so hurt in all my life. I got so tired of his watch-dogging me – never being trusted. I finally had all I could take from him – I got the heck up outta there. I am now living the life of a carefree sister just waiting for the Lord to send someone worthy of me and the love I have to give."

Sistah # 6: "I let the lure of the big bucks blind me! I thought he was the best thing since home-made apple pie. I was a young immature wannabe woman who grew up much too fast. Too many children, too many promises and too much drama for me to realize I was not living the life God destined for me. After many years of marriage to this hustling, con artist, I was too far gone into his world to know what was in my best interest. The lives of me and my children were portraits of the good life to the outside world but behind closed doors, there lurked a monster. In God's time however, I emerge to be the woman of character God always knew I could be and the best is yet to come!"

Sistah # 7: "I don't know why I was fool enough to take his abuse for so many years. Never a commitment to me to help take care of all those children I had with him. I guess my self-esteem was much too low because I thought he loved me. The day he told me to kiss his azz, was the day I knew I was better than that and I took my life back. I struggled but you know what, my God is able to do all things and thanks be to Him, we survived without him."

WHY THEY DON'T TELL

Ever wonder why our daughters, our nieces, our sisters, our granddaughters and our friends' little girls, even our little boys never share their secrets? Do you know why they are afraid of things that go "bump in the night?"

They are afraid to tell because they think no one will ever believe them; they don't tell because they don't want to lose the love of those entrusted to care for them; they don't tell because they think their parents will kill those predators and be sent to jail. They don't tell because they think it's their fault; they don't tell because they're young and vulnerable and think that it is normal for those "monsters" to touch them.

Somebody better listen to those precious babies – when they say they don't like Uncle Bobby - you better listen to them because they have a story to tell. You better dig a little deeper and find out why one of those uncles, brothers, cousins and other relatives or friends in the family are not liked by your beautiful little prince or princess.

Yes baby, there are monsters in your room but they don't always hide in your closet or underneath your bed. So when did Cousin Bobby start to come around? Okay, so when you told Mama he touched you she didn't believe you right? I know mamas are supposed to protect you but just maybe, she sees monsters under her bed (hidden in the psyche of her mind)!

Monsters in her life that were disguised as controlling husbands who were physically and mentally abusive! Monsters who showed up as auntie's husband who wanted to peck her on her cheek with those disgusting wet kisses!

Monsters who winked at her in church who gave her an "innocent" pat on her little behind; Monsters from school disguised as teachers who came by her house when mama was at work! So did I name all those monsters that go "bump in the night"?

Well maybe yes and maybe no because sometimes they are so smooth, you never realize you are having an encounter with a real live monster until the damage has been done.

CHANGE YOUR NAME

Girl what is wrong with you? Why do you answer to a name that does not define who you are? What would happen if a complete stranger came up to you on the street and addressed you as *"bitch, or ho"?* Now be truthful, you know you would go ballistic. You would completely flip out. You would be ready to declare war. Then tell me, why do you let someone who claim to love you, cherish you – who may even be the father of your children, call you those names? Could it be that you are looking for love at any cost? Don't you know how to love yourself and tell that misguided brotha that you are not any of those things he insists on calling you?

Stop answering to those names and start naming yourself according to what Scripture says about you: *Psalm 139:14 declares, "... I am fearfully and wonderfully made; your works are wonderful, I know that full well."* The context of this verse is the incredible nature of our physical and spiritual bodies. The human body is unique, the most complex organism in the world, and that complexity and uniqueness speaks volume about the mind of its Creator. Every aspect of the body, down to the tiniest microscopic cell, reveals that it is fearfully and wonderfully made so how can something that is so wonderfully and fearfully made be treated like trash?

Donald Lawrence speaks to you in his song, "I Speak Life to You."

"I speak life, you gonna live oh my sister. Fight for your life, you shall live and not die!"

My sistah, I speak death to all those events that keep your spirit bound because God wants to do a wonderful thing in your life. However, you must rise up and see yourself forgiven, born again and made into a brand new creature. A saint -- not a bitch! A woman of purpose -- not a ho! A beautiful woman full of possibilities – not a baby mama slut. *Do you hear me girl?* Lift yourself up outta that coma and run with all you have because you don't have much time. You must run the race until you finish your course.

I affirm you my sistah, I lift you up and in so doing - I also lift myself! I bind up all those negative earth-shattering and life-changing situations of our past, and I loose beautiful blessings -- ankles free of shackles so we can dance.

Oh don't pretend you don't know that those broken promises, broken hearts (more than once); broken relationships; wounded spirits as a result of abuse; homelessness, you name it - can keep you bound! But, you can be free with God's help, He can set you free like no other can. He wants to lift you up and you will be close to the Light that is able to *keep* you lifted up. **Romans 8:37 declares, "But despite all this, overwhelming victory is ours through Christ who loved us enough to die for us".**

I want you to remember what Proverbs 18:21 tell us: "**The tongue has the power of life and death.**" Our tongues can build us and others up, or they can tear down. During our conversations and interactions, let's make sure we are building/lifting up –vs- tearing down or belittling. Are you going to trust the Light in spite of what you may be going through and speak life to yourself? **Maurette Brown Clark, reminds us in a song that "It A'int Over" till God says it's over".**

You are also encouraged in the song: "You'll Never Walk Alone" (Lyrics by Rodgers & Hammerstein) "When you walk through a storm, hold your head up high and don't be afraid of the dark. At the end of the storm, there's a golden sky and the sweet silver song of a lark. Walk on through the wind walk on through the rain, though your dreams be tossed and blown. Walk on, walk on, with hope in your hearts and you'll never walk alone - You'll never walk alone!"

Years ago, while studying literature, I was fascinated by the story of the mythological, bird, the Phoenix. A universal symbol of the sun, mystical rebirth, resurrection and immortality, this legendary red "fire bird" was believed to die in its self-made flames periodically (each hundred years, according to some sources) then rise again out of its own ashes.

So what does the story of the Phoenix have to do with your walk? I'm glad you asked! With God's help, you have the power to rise from the ashes of your old life – you have the power to make a miraculous comeback! You have the power to walk through life even though your dreams may be delayed. You are loved Zuri Ntombi (beautiful lady) now rise up with your new name (Child of the Most High God) and take your rightful place in the universe – walk into the Light and rise like that mythological bird the Phoenix!

I have risen from the ashes and it didn't take me 100 years!

BRIDGES

"BRIDGES"

By SADADDY

Excerpt: " Some bridges are meant for light loads; while others are meant for heavy loads; Life is a process of crossing bridges; ... wherever it is or where it may lead you -- cross it – without fear or hesitation." **(Published, 2007 by Life Poetry)**

BRIDGES CAN TAKE YOU MANY PLACES

Edmund Pettus Bridge - Selma, Alabama

This Bridge Took A lot Of People To Some Very Cruel & Vicious Places. But At The End of The Day, Those People Were A Part Of A Great Movement That Would Forever Change Our Country And Paint Our History With A Different Stroke Of The Brush!

****

Golden Gate Bridge – San Francisco, California

This Is One Of The Most Beautifully Structured Bridges In The World But One Of The Most Deadly. It is Reported That Between 1934 and 2012, Over 1400 People Jumped to Their Death From The Bridge. My Point Is – Some Things Can Be So Beautiful, Yet They Can Have Such Pain Associated With Them. However, When We Look Through Different Lenses, We Are Able To See Things From A Different Perspective.

NOTE: I've crossed some very deep waters that could only be reached by sturdy bridges; some of those bridges have been laden with challenges but through perseverance and my abiding faith in God, I managed to make it across every one of them because He redeemed me and now I am ready to cross any bridge that I encounter!

GHANA AT A GLANCE

On a two-week mission trip to Ghana, West Africa, in July of 2008, I kept reminding myself of how blessed I am to live in America! The group led by the Rev. S. L. Thigpen, pastor of Beulah First Baptist Church of Ft. Walton Beach, Florida, arrived in the capital city of Accra, Ghana on the 8th of July.

The population was around 3.5 million (Ghana boasts a population of about 22 million) with the official language being English, but the language most often spoken in that region is GA. There are 65 different ethnic groups occupying Ghana; Christianity is the predominant religion with about 15% of the population embracing Islam. The average life span of Ghana's people is 65 due to the backbreaking hard work (a 65 year old is equivalent to an 80-year-old American).

The poverty level in Ghana is very high and living conditions are very, very bad. Average wages at that time were approximately $15 per month for blue-collar workers; a general physician could expect to earn $250 with specialists earning about $500. If you are fortunate enough to work for the government, you can expect to earn about $150.

Seeing the poverty in Ghana, was very overwhelming; it made me feel very sad – seeing a land that is rich in natural resources (there was a gold mine about a mile down the road from where we were staying) yet villagers still live in thatched roof huts.

Education is a luxury in Ghana; most of the students attend private schools because there are very few government run schools (30-40% of children do not attend school due to extreme poverty).

Pastor Thigpen, delivered an inspirational message from Psalm 27 on Sunday, 13 July, encouraging everyone to have faith because "Jesus is our joy and our strength; He loves us and will always see us through." During the worship service, my heart was overflowing with joy seeing the praise of the people, even though they were living in poverty, they sang with fervency, "God is blessing me and He has plans for my life – it will come true."

A visit to the area's only hospital was very heart wrenching. The hospital had 60 beds and also served as an outpatient facility. There were three doctors to accommodate about 200-300 persons per day. I was moved to tears seeing the conditions under which the hospital had to operate (one used microscope, one old washer and dryer, and a very old x-ray machine).

Upon seeing a pregnant woman awaiting her turn to be served, it was hard to contain my emotions. This woman was beautiful, very neatly dressed and well groomed. However, there was sadness in her eyes; yet there was a glimmer of hope in her smile as I said to her, "blessings upon your baby."

When I look back at my childhood years, I remember how my mother was able to persevere through all the hard times. There were times I know she wanted to give up but there was something inside her that told her, she didn't have the luxury of giving up. My mother was built from tough stock (much like *her* mother). There was a drive inside my mother that put the needs of her children, above her own. My mother would often tell me that I was her last hope and I knew when she told me that, she was remembering all the dreams she had to forego for her family.

Through me, she knew that she could claim victory of having a higher education, of accomplishing things she never had the opportunity to pursue. So, you see, my mother was willing to sacrifice through working from "can to can't" and proving that hard work "never killed nobody."

That pregnant woman was no exception. Her face told me that she was not a quitter; that she had dreams for her child's future. I could tell that the impending arrival of her baby would be a new beginning - - a fresh chapter in her story of perseverance.

Every once in a while, I think about my trip to Africa and I am reminded of my new beginning! You see, as a born-again, new creature in Christ, I am a woman of endurance; a woman of perseverance; a woman who is not a quitter; a woman who lives with hope every day; a woman who has shed many tears - but in the grand scheme of things, I am a woman of great faith who still has dreams and hope for a glorious future!

I am so glad MoDear was not a quitter. Thanks be to God she had dreams for her children and she was blessed to see some of those dreams come to fruition!

BRIDGING THE GAP THROUGH FRIENDSHIP

CO-WORKERS LIFTING VIRGINIA UP ON 04/26/2007

Dear Ms. Virginia

It has been such a pleasure getting to know you. I admire your faithfulness and value your stories, words of wisdom and experience. You will truly be missed. I pray God's blessings in your life and a very happy future. Love, Wanda

Mrs. Virginia

It has been nice working with you, it has been a blessing getting to know you. As I stated yesterday, you have so much wisdom and I really try to draw from that. Although your season was short here, you are leaving such a mark and impression that will not be forgotten. I wish you well and I pray that God will continue to watch over and guide you in your daily walk. Be blessed.
Love, Dominique

Dear Virginia, I'll miss you coming by my desk with words of encouragement. I think your singing was wonderful (SMILE) and I'll really miss that. Where ever you go, I know you'll take good 'karma' because that's how you are. Love, Loretta

---

Ms. Virginia,

WOW! You will be missed so much. It has been a pleasure meeting and knowing you. You are such a blessing in my life. I will miss the conversations, the laughter and the wisdom. Don't worry too much about me; I will be okay. I got the BC and RC Cola by my side :>) - You are a phenomenal woman. I dedicate this poem to you my friend. Take great care of yourself my friend. I will truly miss you!! Much love, Bonita

---

Dear Virginia,
I wish you were not leaving so soon, but believe me – I understand. You are a very pleasant and funny girl (lady). I enjoyed you living on my "row". Hopefully, the next neighbor is as cool as you are. Keep in touch and take care. Love, Patty

---

Ginger My Sister: Remember? I will miss you so much so I will adapt to a new arrival time of 8-4:30. May God speed and you keep in touch! Juanita

---

Virginia,

"Those who dream by day are cognizant of many things which escape those who dream only by night." Stay strong my sister and although it's been a short time knowing you, it's been a pleasure. Desmond

---

Ms. Virginia, I've enjoyed working with you and I will miss seeing your happy face. You have been kind to me and I appreciate that. Take care and God Bless you. Love, Darren

---

Virginia, May your Creator bring you great blessings while guiding your path through the next and future stages of life after federal Government. Live your moments thrilled with the happiness of each breath of life knowing you are loved and cherished. Whatever your future endeavors, keep your head to the sky. Wish we could have had times to really talk and share. God bless & keep you! Joe

---

Virginia, as I read some of the beautiful words your co-workers and friends wrote to you, I was overwhelmed. How wonderful to have created such a loving impact on us in such a short period. You are truly a special person and I wish you all the best life has to offer as you begin your new venture. Be happy, healthy and blessed. Love, Fannie

---

Virginia, Best wishes to you in all your endeavors! Although your stay with us has been "short" you have touched many. Our memories of you will long be remembered. Good luck! Linda

---

I will miss you dearly. Sherran

My prayer for you ... May God bless and keep you and give you peace. May His richest blessings be yours! Peace be within your walls, prosperity within your palaces and peace within you always. May your work in the ministry prosper and grow according to God's plans for you. Deborah

---

GOING HOME

The day my mother wrote me a letter, telling me she was afraid to stay in her home because she was hearing rats in the wall, she was afraid to be alone, to please come and get her, was the day I knew that her mind was under siege. You see, MoDear had always been very independent. Besides, she was completely deaf – how could she be hearing rats in the wall! However unreal it seemed to me, I would realize later that her fears were indeed real and that the nature of the disease intensified those fears.

As MoDear's illness (Alzheimer's) progressed, I saw her development go in reverse order. Her brain was "peeled away like an onion" as she forgot how to live. The progression became escalated to the point of her needing total care.

Alzheimer's is a very tragic disease and over a period of time MoDear lost all memory of everything she had ever learned over her lifetime, with the exception of one thing (she always remembered the name Jesus)! Isn't that awesome! Here she was, locked inside herself in a virtual prison, most often not able to recognize her family, not able to articulate, but always ever present of the powerful force that lived inside of her – that power being the Holy Spirit/Jesus the Christ!

What an awesome testament to see my mother cling to the knowledge that whatever circumstance or state she was in, she never forget how to call on the name of Jesus!

MoDear existed in a state, totally void of knowledge of very simple things. She forgot how to take care of herself in all areas that the rest of us do out of simple habit. She could not dress, clean, or feed herself. In fact, at some point in the very final stages she didn't even remember how to eat. She just simply existed. It became very difficult for our family when MoDear could no longer recognize us. When this happened, it became very important for us to lift each other up with encouragement and love. We remembered the words she had always told us, **"Do the right thing and love each other. Lift each other up"**!

MoDear always personified love and she was concerned about leaving that legacy of love behind for her family. MoDear showed her family that she was a born-again Christian in every aspect of her life. She was a very giving person and she found time to always share with those who were not as blessed as she was.

MoDear would always tell us, "When I go, I don't want nobody crying over me. If anybody want to act a "fool" just take them outside the church and leave them. There ain't no need to do all that hollering, just treat me right while I'm living.

And another thing, don't put nobody on that program to get up there telling lies (y'all know what I'm talking about, as "a neighbor; as a friend; as a church member). That's why it's important to live so at the end, your life will speak for you – as God knows you."

After MoDear's doctor recommended that it would be a good idea to admit her to hospice care so she could receive around the clock medical care, it was very difficult for us to watch her further waste away. She would sometimes wake up enough to recognize us and tell us she was ready to go "home" and if *I* would let her **go**, she could die. I distinctly remember telling her, "I'm not holding you." To which she replied, yes you are.

After some days passed, it finally sank in with me, that she wanted to be free. On one particular day, she was alert enough for me to write her a note and tell her, **"It's okay, you can go when you are ready."**

After a few days, MoDear started her journey home. The nurses told us, it wouldn't be long. Sitting by her bedside, singing to her and holding her hand, I could feel the life ebbing away as her body started to get cold. That was probably one of the most difficult days of my life – seeing someone I loved so deeply, leave me.

However, God in His infinite wisdom, knew she was tired of suffering and He was sparing us the agony of seeing her suffer any longer. Slowly, Modear took flight as I could hear that raspy sound of death take over her frail and weakened body! At that moment, I could feel God lifting her up into His arms and I could feel MoDear lifting me up -- like a heavy weight had been lifted from my shoulders. ***SHE IS GONE!***

REDEMPTION

Redemption is defined as an act of atoning for a fault or mistake, or the state of being rescued, or delivered from sin; having salvation through faith in Jesus the Christ. On the cross, Jesus took the punishment I deserved for my sin. He did not deserve to die, but He willingly took my place and experienced death for me. **(1 Peter 3:18)** explains ... "For Christ also suffered once for sins, the righteous for the unrighteous, that he might bring us to God, being put to death in the flesh but made alive in the spirit." (English Standard Version –ESV)

I am so glad that God loved me enough to send His only Son to be the "go between" for me. Without the shedding of Jesus' blood on the cross, I would still be a wretched mess. Instead of spending eternity in the burning lake of fire (hell), I am now destined for eternal life in heaven with my Lord and Savior Jesus the Christ and I can truly say in the words of the popular hymn, "I Am Redeemed" by Jessy Dixon.

"I am redeemed, bought with a price, Jesus has changed my whole life. If anybody asks you, just who I am, tell them I am redeemed. Where there is hate, love now abides, where there was confusion, peace now reigns. I'm a child, child of the King, it's all because I am redeemed".

Psalm 56:8-13 - The Message Bible: "You've kept track of my every toss and turn through the sleepless nights. Each tear entered in your ledger, each ache written in your book. I'm proud to praise God. Fearless now, I trust in God; what can mere mortals do to me? God, you did everything you promised, and I'm thanking you with all my heart. You pulled me from the brink of death, my feet from the cliff-edge of doom. Now I stroll at leisure with God in the sunlit fields of life".

Just as David cried out to God in this Psalm, I also cried out feeling that in my darkest nights God was nowhere to be found. However, this Psalm reminds me that every tear I cried, God was aware of every one and he was there all the time – waiting to raise me up like He did Lazurus.

He called me forth to witness to other Sistahs who don't know they can make it out! I can still hear Him telling me, **"pick up your bed and be made whole – healed of fear, healed of intimidation, healed of everything that will keep you from witnessing my love.** God, I thank you for your redeeming grace and I thank you for never ever giving up on me. If anybody asks me, just who I am, I will forever tell them – **I AM REDEEMED – BOUGHT WITH A PRICE!**

ABOUT THE AUTHOR

Virginia "Jenny" Hall-Broadnax was born in Union Springs, Alabama and later moved to Chicago, Illinois where she graduated from high school and college. She has also lived in Miami, Atlanta, and currently lives in Fort Walton Beach, Florida. This is Virginia's first published work but she has considered herself a writer for many years.

Virginia loves motivational speaking, and is inspired by young people and the elderly. Virginia's specific ministry calling is working with young people to help them build dreams.

She retired from the Federal Government as an EqualOpportunity Housing Investigator from the Department of Housing and Urban Development (HUD); is a graduate of Roosevelt University in Chicago with a Bachelor's Degree in Communications; received a Master's Degree in Practical Ministry from the Masters International University of Divinity in Evansville, Indiana.

My MoDear always wanted her life to be remembered for her steadfastness in the WORD, and her total reliance on the LOVE OF GOD. I will always be grateful to a mother who loved me, trained me, and didn't give up on me and for **ALWAYS** Lifting Me Up to God, through her prayers, supplication and instruction!

When you think you can't go another second, another minute, another hour, another day, another week, another month, or another year, just look at yourself in the mirror and say, I love you, God loves you and He will never ever separate you from His love. Tell yourself how you made it over hills and mountains and how you made it through valleys low. Keep encouraging yourself until the narrative changes and you're finally able to walk with your head up, shoulders squared and walk on into your destiny.

Remind yourself that your faith brought you thus far, your hope is built upon the knowledge that Jesus died for you. Keep telling yourself that He lifted you with His love and now you are equipped to tell others about His abiding love and redemption!

EPILOGUE

Mrs. Julia Mae Tolbert Hall was born in Bullock County, Alabama on December 5, 1906 to the late Robert and Mary Tolbert. She went home to be with her Lord and Savior Jesus Christ on October 26, 1995. MoDear was united in matrimony on March 11, 1934 to Clarence Hall and to this union, four daughters were born.

MoDear was converted at a very early age and joined the Hardaway A.M.E. Church where she served until uniting with Mt. Zion Baptist Church, Union Springs, Alabama. She was also a member of Mt. Olive M.B. Church, Chicago, Illinois; Beulah First Baptist Church, Ft. Walton Beach, Florida and Solid Rock M.B. Church; Decatur, Georgia, where she was a faithful member until her health failed.

MoDear had a kind and giving spirit and she always strived to make her life and the lives of her loved ones more successful. She was born, she lived, she died and now she lives again and we, who are left behind, will continue to lift up her memory in a very positive way. MoDear's spirit is a part of us and we remember her with love, appreciation and pride for her unselfish devotion to her family and friends. She always found time to lift me up and through her vision for me, I believe I can reach the unreachable (with God on my side, there is no stopping me). Arrogance? No Way! I have learned that **"the harvest truly is plenteous, but the laborers are few. Matthew 9:37 (KJV)**

BIBLIOGRAPHY

Holy Bible (KJV)

Women of Color Study Bible

Life Application Study Bible

Easy to Read Bible

The Message Bible

Bible - English Standard Version (ESV)

<u>INSPIRATIONAL QUOTES</u>

"FOR IN THE END, FREEDOM IS A PERSONAL AND LONELY BATTLE; AND ONE FACES DOWN FEARS OF TODAY SO THAT THOSE OF TOMORROW MIGHT BE ENGAGED."
Alice Walker

===

"ONE CAN NEVER CONSENT TO CREEP WHEN ONE FEELS THE IMPULSE TO SOAR." Helen Keller

"DANCE IS THE HIDDEN LANGUAGE OF THE SOUL."
Martha Graham

"WE MAY ENCOUNTER MANY DEFEATS BUT WE MUST NOT BE DEFEATED."   Maya Angelou

"GIVE LIGHT AND PEOPLE WILL FIND THE WAY." Ella Baker

"WE CHOOSE OUR JOYS AND SORROWS LONG BEFORE WE EXPERIENCE THEM." Khalil Gibran

NOBODY TO LIFT ME

This book is not meant to portray my life as one of gloom and doom nor to boast, but rather to attest to the fact that through God's *Amazing Grace* He has made the difference in my life.

I now realize that I had to take the journey I did in order for God to prepare me for the place I needed to be. My life has PURPOSE and just like the story of Shadrach, Meshach and Abednego, I was never alone in the "fiery furnace."

AND SO IT IS

Made in the USA
Columbia, SC
25 October 2021